International Food Library

FOOD IN
RUSSIA

International Food Library

FOOD IN
RUSSIA

Tania Andreev

Rourke Publications, Inc.
Vero Beach, Florida 32964

Library of Congress Cataloging-in-Publication Data

Andreev, Tania, 1935-
   Food in Russia/by Tania Andreev.
     p. cm. - (International food)
   Summary: Surveys food products, customs, and preparation in the Soviet Union, describing regional dishes, cooking techniques, and recipes for a variety of meals.
   ISBN 0-86625-343-2
   1. Cookery, Russian - Juvenile literature. 2. Food habits - Soviet Union - Juvenile literature. 3. Soviet Union - Social life and customs - Juvenile literature. [1. Cookery, Russian. 2. Food habits - Soviet Union. 3. Soviet Union - Social life and customs.] I. Title. II. Series. International food series.
TX723.3.A53 1989
394. 1'0947-dc19   88-32179
                   CIP
                   AC

CONTENTS

AN INTRODUCTION TO RUSSIA

Russia is by far the largest member of the Union of Soviet Socialist Republics (U.S.S.R.), sometimes called the Soviet Union. Because the Russian Republic dominates the Soviet Union geographically, politically, and economically, the U.S.S.R. is often mistakenly referred to as Russia.

The Soviet Union was established as a result of the Russian Revolution in 1917, when factory workers, soldiers, and peasants overthrew the government of the ruler, Czar Nicholas II. A communist government was set up, which is today led by Mikhail Gorbachev. Initially the Soviet Union consisted of the republics of Russia, Ukraine, Belorussia and Transcaucasia, but it expanded over the years to its present membership of fifteen republics.

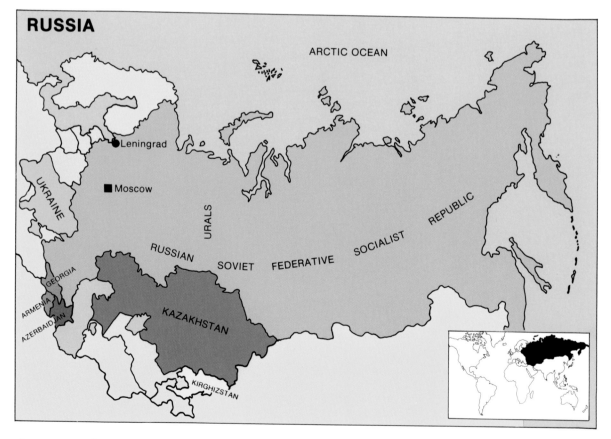

Russia is the most industrially developed republic in the Soviet Union.

Today the Soviet Union is the largest country in the world, stretching for 8.65 million square miles across the northern part of the European/Asian continent. The Soviet Union has nearly 300 million people, more than half of whom originate from the Russian Soviet Federal Socialist Republic. At 6.59 million square miles — roughly equal in size to the United States — Russia occupies just over three-quarters of the total land area of the Soviet Union and is its most powerful republic.

Russia is a rich republic, accounting for around 70 percent of the Soviet Union's industrial and agricultural production. The republic has great natural resources, including oil and gas, coal, iron ore, lead, tin, copper, zinc, gold, and platinum. Russia's capital city, Moscow, is also the capital of the Soviet Union and the seat of government.

AGRICULTURE IN RUSSIA

The Soviet Union is a leading agricultural nation. Its timber reserves are the largest in the world; it is the second largest producer of pigs and cattle and has the world's second largest fishing fleet. This position of leadership is, of course, largely due to the immensity of the country, rather than the efficiency of the Soviet Union's agricultural system. Although much progress has been made over the last sixty years, the Soviets feel there are still many improvements to make.

The Soviet Union has always placed great importance on its agricultural strength, since it has a considerable effect on the country's economy. Today the Soviet Union is trying hard to become self-sufficient in agriculture, so it will not have to import food from other countries. Plans are under way to increase production by over 14 percent between 1986 and 1989. To achieve this, the government has made many changes in agricultural policy and farming methods.

Russia has the world's second largest fishing fleet.

A helicopter brings visitors to a reindeer farm in the north of Russia.

Since the late 1920s almost every farm in the Soviet Union has been owned by the state. Collective farms, *kolkhoz*, are government-owned but run by elected officials with farm workers from one or more villages. Profits are shared by the workers according to the work they have put into the farm. The much larger state farms, *sovkhoz*, are owned and run by the state.

The Soviet Union has recognized that farm workers need some incentive to increase agricultural output. The government has recently introduced bonuses for meeting production targets, and farm workers are now allowed to form groups to rent and farm land for themselves. City dwellers have been encouraged to cultivate garden plots to grow their own fruit and vegetables and even to farm livestock. This has increased production in that sector by around 12 percent.

9

FOOD IN RUSSIA

The Russians are some of the most hospitable people in the world. They love to gather together for tea around a boiling samovar or to share a food-laden table with their family or friends. Even when people show up unexpectedly, they are given the warmest welcome and invited to join in the next meal. The Russians have a special word for hospitality: *khlebosol'stvo.* This comes from the Russian tradition of offering bread *(khleb)* and salt *(sol')* to visitors upon their arrival.

A lady in Russian dress brings the traditional greeting of bread and salt.

This brightly painted market stall is selling bread and cookies.

The climate in over half of the Russian republic is too cold for growing food, and the northern parts are used for forestry and reindeer farming. All the food comes from the warmer central and southern regions, which supply the staple foods such as wheat, potatoes, vegetables, beef, pork, and dairy produce. These foods are sold either in state-owned supermarkets or at the more popular, but sometimes expensive, markets. The markets usually offer a wider choice of goods, with stalls selling freshly baked bread, biscuits, and pies as well as meat and vegetables. Large refrigerators are not common in the Soviet Union, so people must shop every day.

Russian cuisine varies from the wholesome one-course peasants' meal of a thick soup or stew served with bread and pickles to a full dinner with a selection of dishes. A full dinner would normally begin with *zakuski*, a selection of beautifully presented cold dishes that can be either simple or elaborate. The *zakuski* may include something very expensive, like caviar, or may be a colorful but less exotic array of cold meats, fish, and salads. A meat or fish dish follows, and the meal is completed by tea or coffee served with a selection of Russian cakes and biscuits or desserts.

WHEAT

Scientists believe that wheat was one of the first cereal crops people ever cultivated. Wheat is an easy crop to grow and can be stored for long periods as long as it is cool, dry, and clean. It has become the most widely grown and used crop, occupying one-sixth of the world's total area of cultivated land. Wheat accounts for almost one-half of Russia's total grain production and is its most important crop, providing the staple food for millions of people. Russians eat a lot of bread and serve it with every meal.

Wheat is an important crop in Russia; it is cultivated over large areas of the Soviet Union.

Harvesting the wheat crop in the vast central plains.

Wheat is grown in the central plains, to the east of the Ural Mountains, and in the far southeasterly corners of Russia close to the Chinese border. The other very important wheat-growing areas of the Soviet Union are northern Kazakhstan and the Ukraine - sometimes referred to as the bread basket of the U.S.S.R. The area of land under wheat cultivation has doubled since 1913, but the Soviet Union is able to produce only about three-quarters of the wheat it needs.

The Soviet Union currently imports nearly 30 million tons of grain each year. In years when the harvest is poor, the Soviet Union must import millions more tons of grain to feed its people. This not only means that the country must pay a lot more for its food, but it must also be dependent on other nations for basic necessities. Following the Soviet invasion of Afghanistan in 1979, President Carter refused to sell more than the minimum amount of grain previously agreed upon to the Soviet Union. This meant the Soviets had to buy smaller quantities of grain wherever they could, resulting in rationing and long and exhausting lines for bread.

POTATOES

From their humble beginnings in the mountains of the northern Andes range in South America, potatoes have become one of the world's eight most important foods. They had been cultivated in South America for at least 1,400 years before the Spaniards introduced them to Europe in the second half of the sixteenth century. By the nineteenth century potatoes were firmly established as a major European food crop.

Today the Soviet Union grows over one-quarter of the world's potatoes. One of the main growing areas is around the city of Moscow in the western half of the Russian Republic, but smaller quantities are cultivated on farms and private plots all over the Soviet Union.

People who work on collective and state farms are given the opportunity to farm small 1.25 acre plots of land for themselves. Nearly all the workers take advantage of this, using their land to raise livestock or grow vegetables. Approximately 60 percent of the Soviet Union's potatoes are grown on these individual plots.

Russians are so fond of potatoes that they sometimes call them "the second bread." There are several different recipes for potato salads that form part of the *zakuski* table, and potatoes are often found in thick Russian soups and stews. Sub-standard potatoes are never wasted but are given instead to the livestock as animal feed.

About one-fifth of the potatoes grown in Russia are processed. They may be canned or frozen, or even distilled to make vodka. Vodka is an alcoholic drink that is very popular in Russia. In fact, according to studies, so much vodka was being drunk in the Soviet Union that it was damaging people's health. The government decided to take measures to stop people from drinking so much vodka. In 1984 they began to close down the distilleries where vodka was made, and their production has now fallen by one-half. The Soviet Union is still, however, able to export nearly 90,000 gallons of vodka to the rest of the world.

Russians are very fond of potatoes, which are grown all over the Soviet Union.

14

REGIONAL COOKING

With a population including over one hundred different ethnic groups, the Soviet Union has a wide range of cooking styles and ingredients. Food that is common in one part of the Soviet Union may be very hard to find in another region, or the people living there may simply not like it. A Leningrader probably would not enjoy fermented mare's milk any more than a Kirghizian peasant would appreciate the subtle flavor of the best caviar, and not many Russians share the Soviet Eskimos' taste for raw fish!

The southern republics of Georgia, Armenia, and Azerbaidjan often cook fish on outdoor barbecues.

Mikhail Gorbachev, leader of the Soviet Union, visits a sheep farm in Uzbekhistan; lamb is often on the menu in this republic.

Food in the northerly regions of the Soviet Union is designed to keep out the cold winter chills. Red meat, potatoes, and other root vegetables are made into warming soups and casseroles. Wheat does not grow well in these northern areas, and black rye bread is a satisfying accompaniment to a meal. Steaming dumplings are stuffed with beef and pork and spiced with hot mustard. Cattle thrive on the rich pastures of the Baltic republics, so food there is always served with dollops of cream, butter, cheese, and milk. *Smetana*, or sour cream, and *tvorog*, or curd cheese, are typically Russian dairy products that are used in great quantity.

The republics of Georgia, Armenia, and Azerbaidjan bask in the warm sunshine of the south. Many exotic fruits and vegetables that are the envy of the northern republics can be grown here. These republics' historic links with the middle eastern countries of Turkey, Iran, and Iraq are reflected in their cuisine. Spices and fresh herbs are important ingredients, and meat, fish, and sweet corn are often cooked over a sizzling charcoal barbecue.

RUSSIAN FESTIVALS

Under the Soviet Union's communist doctrine, religion was originally discouraged, and religious holidays like Christmas and Easter are still not formally recognized. Russia's official national holidays commemorate events that led to the establishment of the Soviet Union, such as Victory Day and Constitution Day.

Probably the most important national holiday, November 7, is the anniversary of the Great October Socialist Revolution of 1917, when the Soviet state was established. In the morning there are huge displays of military strength, as tanks and artillery thunder through Moscow's Red Square. During the afternoon and evening, families gather for festive dinners and enjoy firework displays.

This military display marks the seventieth anniversary of the establishment of the Soviet Union in October 1987.

Many towns in the Soviet Union have their own festivals; these people are taking part in a song festival.

These national holidays, however, lack the traditional elements of which the Russian people are so fond. Although the holidays are times for family parties and outings, only New Year's Day on January 1 is celebrated in a traditional style. Many of the Christmas customs have been adopted for New Year's. A goose or chicken is roasted, and special foods are prepared that were formerly a treat to break the fast on Christmas Eve. Christmas trees have become New Year's trees.

Although some events are no longer celebrated, many traditions related to them have survived. Russians used to mark the arrival of spring with a festival called *Zhavoronki*. Spring was, and still is, eagerly awaited after the long, bitterly cold northern winters. People believed spring began when the larks returned from their migration in early March. To celebrate the arrival of warmer weather, they made sweet rolls in the shape of larks, which still appear in bakeries during the first days of March.

A BANQUET MENU FOR A FESTIVE OCCASION

Russian Egg Salad
Cucumber Salad With Sour Cream
Herring In Mustard Sauce
Beef Stroganov
Strawberry Kissel
Tea Or Coffee With Almond Cookies

The egg, cucumber, and herring salads form the hors d'oeuvres, or *zakuski*. They should be served first, followed by the beef stroganov. Then serve the strawberry kissel before ending the meal with tea or coffee and cookies.

Russian Egg Salad

  3 *hard-boiled eggs, peeled and cut in half*
  3 *firm tomatoes, cut in half*
  ¾ *cup mayonnaise*
  2 *ozs. mushrooms, minced*
  1 *oz. grated cheese*
  1 *oz. ham, minced*
  ¼ *teaspoon minced garlic*
     pinch salt

1. Scoop out the yolks of the hard-boiled eggs. Mix with the mayonnaise, mushrooms, cheese, ham, salt, and garlic.
2. Fill the eggs with the mayonnaise stuffing and top with half a tomato. Serve chilled.

Cucumber Salad With Sour Cream

  1 *cucumber, thinly sliced*
  2 *tablespoon sour cream*
  1 *tablespoon chopped dill*
     pinch salt and pepper

1. Arrange the cucumber in a serving dish and add salt and pepper. Pour over the sour cream.
2. Sprinkle with chopped dill and serve chilled.

Russian Egg Salad.

Herring In Mustard Sauce

    6 pieces pickled herring (or 1 8 oz. jar)
    1 tablespoon olive oil
    1 tablespoon Dijon mustard
    1 tablespoon sour cream
    1 teaspoon capers

1. Mix together the oil and mustard. Add the sour cream and capers.
2. Arrange the herring in a serving dish and pour over the sauce. Serve chilled.

21

Beef Stroganov

    2 lbs. round steak, cut into thin strips
       2 inches long by ½ inch wide
    2 onions, finely chopped
    1 cup beef stock
    ½ cup sour cream
    1 tablespoon Dijon mustard
    1 teaspoon salt
    ½ teaspoon black pepper
    1 teaspoon cornstarch
    2 tablespoons olive oil

1. Heat the oil in a large pan and gently fry the onions and steak for 10 minutes until cooked through.
2. Add the beef stock and salt, and bring to a boil. Mix the cornstarch with a little water and add to thicken the sauce.
3. Stir in the mustard, black pepper, and sour cream, and serve hot.

Strawberry Kissel

    1 lb. strawberries, peeled, cored, and sliced
    2 tablespoons sugar
      juice of ½ lemon
      finely grated peel of ¼ lemon
    1 tablespoon potato flour or cornstarch
    2 cups water
      pinch nutmeg.

Strawberry Kissel.

A Russian samovar with cookies.

1. Pour just enough water into a pan to cover the base. Add the strawberries and sugar and boil until soft and pulpy.
2. Strain the strawberry mixture into a second pan. Add the lemon juice, lemon peel, and nutmeg.
3. Mix the flour with a little water and stir into the strawberry mixture. Bring to a boil and simmer for 5 minutes, stirring continuously. Pour into six dessert dishes and cool before serving.

Almond Cookies

4 ozs. butter
3 ozs. sugar
¾ cup plain flour
1 egg
1 egg yolk
4 tablespoons flaked almonds

1. Lightly beat together the butter and sugar until creamy. Beat in the egg, then lightly stir in the flour to make a dough.
2. Press the dough into a greased 7 inch pie pan. Brush the top with the beaten egg yolk and sprinkle with the flaked almonds.
3. Bake for 15 minutes until golden in an oven pre-heated to 375 degrees.

A GEORGIAN STYLE MEAL

Lamb Kebabs
Georgian Cheese Pie

Kebabs, or *shashlyk*, are a favorite dish from the southern republic of Georgia, as are Georgian cheese pies. Serve both dishes hot, with a bowl of chilled tomatoes, radishes, and green onions.

Lamb Kebabs

1½ lbs. lamb, cut into 2 inch cubes
  2 tablespoons olive oil
  1 teaspoon salt
  1 teaspoon minced garlic
    juice of 1 lemon
  1 lemon, cut into quarters
  4 skewers

1. Place the lamb pieces in a dish. Mix together the remaining ingredients and pour over the lamb. Marinate for 4 hours.
2. Pour off the marinade and thread the pieces of meat onto the skewers to make kebabs.
3. Grill the kebabs on an outdoor barbecue over very hot coals, or place in the oven under the broiler. Using a hot pad, turn the kebabs every few minutes until thoroughly cooked.
4. Serve hot, garnished with lemon wedges.

Georgian Cheese Pie

  ½ lb. plain flour
  1 cup milk
1½ tablespoons dried yeast
  2 ozs. soft butter
  1 teaspoon salt
  ½ lb. grated cheese
  2 eggs
  2 ozs. soft butter

**Lamb Kebabs and
Georgian Cheese Pie.**

1. Heat the milk in a pan until just warm and stir in the dried yeast until dissolved. Add the salt and butter, and stir in the flour bit by bit, mixing well, to make a dough.
2. Using your hands, knead the dough until it is smooth. Place it in a greased bowl and let it rise for about 2 hours.
3. Mix together the remaining butter, grated cheese, and eggs until you have a fairly smooth mixture for the filling.
4. When the dough is ready, divide it into two equal pieces. Using a rolling pin, roll out each piece of dough on a floured board to a circle of just over 12 inches in diameter.
5. Place one piece of dough in a 12-inch pie dish and pour in the cheese filling. Then place the second piece over the top and pinch the edges together.
6. Bake for 40 minutes in an oven preheated to 375 degrees, and serve hot.

A RUSSIAN STYLE MEAL

Russian Beef Casserole
Vegetable Salad

The two dishes that form the basis of this simple Russian meal should be served at the same time. Make the salad first and refrigerate it until the beef is ready.

Russian Beef Casserole

1½ lbs. round steak
  6 medium potatoes, peeled and cut into quarters
  3 turnips, peeled and cut into quarters
  2 onions, chopped
  8 small carrots, peeled and cut into quarters
  2 cups beef stock
  1 cup sour cream
  2 tablespoons tomato paste
  2 tablespoons oil
  1 bay leaf
  1 teaspoon salt
  ½ teaspoon black pepper
  1 teaspoon minced garlic
  2 tablespoons green onions, chopped
  2 tablespoons fresh dill, chopped

1. Heat the oil in a large pan and gently fry the onions, garlic, potatoes, and turnips for about 10 minutes, until lightly browned.
2. Cut the beef into 8 equal slices and add to the pan. Fry for 10 minutes more. Add the beef stock, bay leaf, salt, pepper, and carrots. Cover and simmer for one hour until the beef is tender.
3. Stir in the sour cream and tomato paste. Serve hot, sprinkled with green onions and dill.

**Russian Beef
Casserole and
Vegetable Salad.**

Vegetable Salad

 ½ *head cabbage*
 2 *carrots*
 2 *tablespoons fresh dill, finely chopped*
 4 *tablespoons vinegar*
 2 *tablespoons olive oil*
 1 *teaspoon sugar*
 ½ *teaspoon salt*

1. Wash and finely shred the cabbage and carrots and
    place in a bowl with the dill.
2. Add the vinegar, olive oil, sugar, and salt and mix
    thoroughly. Chill until ready to serve, and then dish
    into four separate salad bowls.

AN EVERYDAY MEAL

The Russians are very fond of thick farmhouse soup, which they consider a meal in itself. The most famous of Russian soups is this satisfying beet soup called borscht. Serve it with thick slices of fresh, hot bread.

Borscht

   1 lb. beef shinbone
   ½ lb. cooked beets, peeled and grated (or 1 8-oz. can)
   2 medium potatoes, peeled and chopped
   1 carrot, peeled and grated
   ½ head cabbage, shredded
   2 large tomatoes, chopped
   1 large onion, thinly sliced
   1 teaspoon sugar
   1 teaspoon salt
   ½ teaspoon black pepper
   1 bay leaf
   2 tablespoons vinegar
   1 cup sour cream
   8 cups water

1. Place the beef in a large pan and add 8 cups of water. Bring to a boil and simmer for 20 minutes to make a meat stock.
2. Add the beets, potatoes, carrot, bay leaf, salt, and pepper and cook for 10 minutes more. Then add the cabbage, onion, tomatoes, sugar, and vinegar and cook for 30 minutes more. Remove from the heat and leave to cool.
3. When cool, remove the meat bone from the pan and strip it of any meat. Put the pieces of meat back into the soup.
4. Place the soup back on the burner and bring to a boil. Serve hot with a generous spoonful of sour cream in each dish.

GLOSSARY OF COOKING TERMS

For those readers who are less experienced in the kitchen, the following list explains the cooking terms used in this book.

Chopped	Cut into small pieces measuring about ½ inch
Finely chopped	Cut into very small pieces measuring about ⅛ inch
Garnished	Decorated
Grated	Rubbed against a grater to produce very small pieces
Greased	Having been lightly coated with oil or margarine to prevent the contents from sticking
Knead	To work a dough with one's hands
Marinate	To let soak up a mixture of juices called a marinade
Minced	Chopped into tiny pieces or put through a mincer
Preheated	Already heated to the required temperature
Shredded	Cut into lengths of 1-2 inches, about ¼ inch across
Finely shredded	As above, but about ⅛ inch across
Strain	Pour through a strainer to remove any large pieces
Simmer	To leave at a low boil
Skewers	Pointed metal or wooden sticks that hold pieces of meat or vegetables in a row to make a kebab
Sliced	Cut into thin pieces that show part of the original shape of the vegetable
Spoon measurements	Tablespoons and teaspoons should be filled only to the level of the spoon's edge, not heaped

RUSSIAN COOKING

To make the recipes in this book, you will need the following special ingredients:

Capers Small green buds or berries sold in jars at most supermarkets.

Dried Yeast Yeast can be bought from any large supermarket.

Herbs Bay leaves and dill are best used fresh. You may be able to find them in the produce section of a supermarket or at a farmers' market. If not, substitute dried herbs or use an alternative fresh herb, such as parsley, that is easier to find.

Oil Olive oil is recommended for cooking Russian foods, especially for recipes from the southern states. If you are serving someone, such as a parent or grandparent, who is on a low-cholesterol diet, be sure to use olive oil or sunflower oil, which do not contain any cholesterol.

Potato flour Some supermarkets carry potato flour on the same shelves as the wheat flour. If you can't find it, substitute cornstarch to thicken sauces.

Spices Nutmeg is sold on the spice rack of all supermarkets.

This table is laid with zakuski.

INDEX

We would like to thank and acknowledge the following people for the use of their photographs and transparencies:

Ardea London Ltd: 15; Ebury Press: 28; Novosti Press Agency: Cover, T/Page, 7, 8/9, 10/11, 12, 12/13, 16/17, 26/27, 24/25, 18/19, 21, 23, 29, 31; Society for Cultural Relations: 22.